Grass Grows in Winter

Pain and Purpose
through the Storm
after the Loss
of a Child

CHERYL WILLIAMS

Fulton Books
Meadville, PA

Published by Fulton Books 2024

ISBN 979-8-88982-874-7 (paperback)
ISBN 979-8-88982-875-4 (digital)

Printed in the United States of America

This book is dedicated to my son, Jordan, and to each and every precious child who left their mark on our world and sadly is no longer with us. May their memories and legacies live on inside of us throughout eternity. We can only be counted as blessed to have had the opportunity of crossing their paths during their lifetime—a time that ended too soon.

Contents

Preface

This book touches on the topic of child loss through a grieving parent's heart. Losing a child is devastating, and over time, a new normal gently eases into their existence that a parent embraces and learns to live. Nothing will ever be the same again in their lives. Sharing that experience and letting others know they are not alone and there is someone out there thinking about them gives comfort to the grieving parent. The goal here is to come to realize that someday they will all be able to say they are going to be okay. It may be months or years down the road, but subtle changes will take place that go unnoticed. Survival is the key to child loss. This book is uplifting and compassionate, written by a brokenhearted parent who has learned to survive and walk this journey no one should be on.

Acknowledgment

Written by me and planted and directed by God. Without Him, this book would not be. I give it all to Him.

An Unfinished Life

My son, Jordan Eugene Williams, was born on November 12, 1985, at 6:42 a.m. to me and my partner, Gary Williams (who later became my husband). It was a Tuesday. He died on November 3, 2008, in a tragic automobile accident in which he was the driver. It was a Monday.

If you are reading this right now and have not lost a child to the ugly face of death, I apologize now for my bluntness. I and many other parents are living proof that, yes, it does happen. Not one of us dreamed in a thousand years that we would bury a child. If I could turn the clock back and save every one of them, I would. I pray not one more parent goes through this. I pray no one else endures what we go through each day of our lives—the turmoil we feel inside, knowing we'll never see our precious child again in this lifetime. The strong, overpowering need we feel to be near our child, to have him back, is beyond words. It is instinctual. Some days are simply too much and unbearable. The pain we experience of this magnitude makes us want life to be over with. We dread going to bed at night if sleep comes at all. We dread getting up in the morning and

1

having to remind ourselves every day, again, that our child is dead. We dread each day as it looms in front of us and wonder how on earth are we going to get through it—another long, sad, lonely day. Every day feels the same. I do not specifically speak for each parent because I know we all experience grief differently from others' grief. No two parents are the same. The processes may be similar with each parent, but one thing I'm sure of, one we can all agree on, is the heart-wrenching feeling of our innermost being, our very heart and soul, which has been shattered to bits, silently crying out for our child.

There are many faces to the grief over the loss of my son. An important one, which I'm sure some can relate to, is the unfinished life of my boy. This is on my mind a lot. So much was lost, or was it? How can I say something was lost if it never was? I often wonder if his future was even written. I guess I believed it was. It is a parent's instinct to believe in a future for his or her child and watch as it comes to fruition.

Nevertheless, this is what we tend to think: that it has all been senselessly lost, forever, a tragedy. We basically tend to write their future from the moment they are born or at least dream of what their future might be and what it holds. This is what we see in our minds. We see time marching on and everyone growing up and growing old like it should be. I call everything, of what we were robbed of or denied, the future what-ifs. It's not fair Jordan didn't get to finish his life, and what if he had? His unfinished life affected mine according to the future I saw, the one

I saw in my mind's eye. Everything was going to be peaches and cream—perfect. What if he were alive today? What if he had lived through that horrible accident? Where and what would he be doing today? I am sad that I'll never know. Just the joy in watching him thrive made all things in my world good.

Sometimes, I paint a picture of it all in my mind, not controlling his life, just watching and wishing for what I see. I wish for all the what-ifs.

At the end of the day, I just so terribly wished he would have had the chance to finish his life. The beauty in a single life lived is beyond words. I wonder, would he be married to the love of his life? This and many other questions are what I wonder about. What kind of a story would his life tell? Would he be living in his dream home? Would he have the career he set his mind to? I see these things in my mind, and they bring a smile to my heart. It's not always sadness; the love I have for him grows stronger.

It is never a bad thing to think about and wish for what could have been. Picturing him as a grown, happy man makes me one proud mama. It brings joy to my heart. It's been many years since Jordan passed, and yet I still wish for the future. I guess I always will. Although I wish for it, I have come to terms with and have accepted the fact that there isn't one for him. But the grass grows and keeps growing around my feet, and the sun keeps shining over my head. Time keeps marching on; therefore, I must move on until we meet again.

I Am

I am in a state of tears, inner pain, and anguish yet surrounded by beauty. Life stretches beyond the loss of a child. The world keeps turning, and inside, I just want to scream from the rooftops to all who can hear me that my child has died. I want them all to stop what they are doing and acknowledge that. I want everyone to pay attention to what I'm saying because somehow, I think that I won't be so alone, alone in carrying this heavy burden by myself, a burden that won't go away or get any lighter with the passing of time. I want help carrying it. I feel singled out, although I know I'm not. I feel like I'm the only one this has happened to, and I know that's not true either. I want the world to stop turning just for a moment so everyone will listen and walk this road with me. I want my son back! I want things to be the way they were, the way it's supposed to be before the world stopped turning for me. Life wasn't supposed to go this way. It's not supposed to be this hard. I know we all have our troubles and our own crosses to bear, but I keep thinking that maybe, just maybe, if my child hadn't died, then my life would be a whole lot easier and that everything would be as it should be. Things would be perfect again. I think that all would be okay and all the troubles would just melt away. This is how I see it; all the hard times and problems in my life stem from this one event. This may not be true for all parents, but maybe it is for some. When things go wrong or a new problem arises, I would think, *If only Jordan hadn't died*, or *If only Jordan were here, things would be as they should*. It could be that I associate bad times with his death, a bad time, a real bad time. I don't claim to know how other parents cope with child loss, but I do know none of us cope with it the same. Your pain is your pain and is different from mine and others. You may have lost a son or a daughter. Your child may have been an infant, a fetus, or a toddler. That toddler may have been a boy or a girl. You may have lost a pre-teen. You may have had a miscarriage and had that child's life in your mind's eye. You may have had a name or even the life picked out for your child. You may have had it all written down in a journal about how happy you were and all your hopes, dreams, and aspirations for that child. In a heartbeat, they vanished—gone. It doesn't matter how many children you have or may not have; one child lost is too many. You may have lost an adult child. This child may have been a grown man or woman with a family of their own. Those hopes and dreams of things to come, things to see of his or her family, just disinte-grated before your very eyes. There's no going back. You can wish it back with all your heart and soul, but it's not coming back. Nothing will ever be the same again for you. You may have lost a daughter, grown and on her own. She was your pride and joy. She may have been all you ever hoped for. You are lost without her now because she is no longer by your side. She may have been your only child. I, too, lost my only child. I am lost without my boy. Jordan was my best friend. Truly, I know you are lost too. You want to be with your child. I have read about parents saying they just want to die or they just want to be with their child. I understand where they're coming from and why they would say that. However, that is not the answer. That's not how it works here on earth. I believe that if I want to see my son again, I must stay here, on earth. I lived for my child when he was alive, and in his death, I still live for him. So please, dear moms and dads, stay.

However it may have happened, the way your precious child died, my deepest and most heartfelt condolences go out to you. My heart and soul reach out to you with the warmest thoughts and prayers for comfort and peace. I know this doesn't always come. Be kind to yourself above all else. I don't claim to know how you feel, but as I stated earlier, your pain is your pain, and no two people are the same during the grieving process. I do know all about that deep-down empty feeling in the pit of your stomach, that feeling of dread and the ghosts of our worst nightmares come to life. This is the feeling that never goes away, the horrendous pain and heartbreak of burying your child and arranging, and attending, a funeral you certainly never dreamed, in a thousand years, you would be at, at least not in your lifetime. It's unnatural watching it all happen as if it weren't really happening, that all of this wasn't really real, trying to decipher it all as it is taking place and how unbelievable it all is. In the back of your mind, all you can do is scream. "WHY? WHY?" From here, you just go numb. Your emotions shut down. You become emotionally bankrupt. You don't care about anything anymore. You don't care about anyone except for that child you just buried. You want to quit your job, quit your life, and anything else you had going on that was good. There is no you anymore. You have been forever changed into someone you don't know mentally or emotionally. You will never be the same you again, the one person you were when your child was alive, the you, you used to be. That person has ceased to exist, the you, you were when the world was spinning properly and your child was alive. The world never stopped, and we are angry as hell, angry at people who keep on living and angry at the life that seems to keep going on even though we are stuck on day one of this journey through hell. We are angry at everything, just not showing it. It's like our insides had been taken out, twisted and beaten to a pulp, and tortured and then put back inside of us and then told to go on, live your life like nothing happened— not possible! I think back on how I felt inside during those early days of my grief. I was angry, quietly, at others for not knowing or for just going on with their lives at a normal pace when here I was, all wrecked on the inside, barely functioning. I was doing all I could to just make it through each minute while trying to come up with a good plan on how to make it through the next. I had no clue how I was going to cope with life from here on out.

The five words no parent wants to hear and yet most people want to say is, "You're going to be okay." I may be wrong telling you you're going to be okay, but I think at the end of the day, we begin to realize that we will be. Life seems very hopeless right now. Sometimes, I wonder what being okay really means. I go to work, I interact with others, I do my job, and I come home. The minute I leave that environment, the blanket comes down, and my mind and soul are exhausted. My mind takes me to another place where sadness lives. The life lost goes through my mind that could have been, had Jordan lived. It's a given; this is here to stay. Each day is a rerun of the one before. I think the same things over and over again. I have learned to live with it. I guess this is my new normal. I'm sure there is a multitude of things I am not saying or thinking here to a recently bereaved parent. My heart goes out to you in ways you may come to understand as you travel your own journey of grief. Grief comes in stages and waves, and we all learn new coping strategies and skills along this dreadful walk, each in our own gentle ways. We learn who we are all over again and are forced to reevaluate our lives. We are not who we once were, and so therefore, we must learn to live with who we are now. Some may argue that we are the same people, but deep down, we have changed dramatically. Sure, I have the same family, extended family members, and friends, and, of course, I still look the same. I live in the same environment (minus my child), but I'm not the same. Others may look at me and see no changes, but seriously, I don't act the same, and I don't think or react or care about things the way I used to. I now care more about things, the important things. Things have more meaning to me now. I love harder. Things are clearer to me now. Life is more precious now, and, yes, I could sit in the forest and stare at a pine tree all day and just be in awe of it. How can such a tall, skinny hunk of a trunk, with its green pine needles and long spindly branches reaching out into space, catch my gaze and hold it there? Maybe it's because it truly is beautiful. Maybe it's God's way of decorating the land, and the trees are just a blanket. Maybe it's my way of slowing down and appreciating the beauty around me more. Maybe it really is a beautiful thing; I just didn't notice it before.

My child was made of beauty. I'll never see him again on this earth. I remember well what he looked like, of course. Through my eyes, his face never changed. He was always *my Jordan*. He still is and will forever be a part of me. He's just not here where he belongs. Over time I have learned to live with that. I am not happy about it. Of course, I never will be. None of us will ever be okay with losing our child, our perfect, in our eyes, beautiful, loving children who were so violently ripped from our seemingly picture-perfect lives. I've learned being angry is not being kind to me. I need to be number one in my own life if I am to survive. You need to be number one in your life. I know there are those of us who have jobs to go to, and maybe you have a family to take care of, but you matter still. You are enough. You may think you are worthless, and some of you shoulder the blame. Stop it! This is not your fault! It will take months, even years, to get where you want or need to be. Beating yourself up won't help. You may think you will never get there, and then one day, you feel as though you have arrived. You will have a feel-good day that makes you stop and think about how far you've come. You'll stop and ponder about all you have learned along this mandatory journey. You will feel good about yourself again, I promise. When we try to stop the sadness and gather up our sanity to go on, we find that it is a little easier each time. Being okay doesn't mean you have betrayed your child or yourself. It doesn't mean that you have moved eons away from their memory. That is something that will never go away. You will always have them with you, inside of you. We don't have to stay in a constant state of grief and pain. We will always grieve our child. I choose to embrace the life my child lived and not be controlled by pain and sadness. I choose to grow because where I was gave me no choice. I didn't sign up for nor did I buy a seat on this train, but I do know there is more to me inside, more of me that I don't know about, and I want to know what it is. There's more to me than anticipating bedtime and then dreading getting up in the morning because I know I will have to stumble through another pain-filled day. I know I will have to put on that face again. I must exist and face the world every day without my child by my side. I know there's more to me than this. I am not belittling the fact that my child died or anyone else's. What I want out of life is what my child would have wanted for me—*to live*. I know there's more to me than this. THIS is the death of my son. THIS is the sadness, the sorrow, the grief, and all that come along with it that I never wanted. None of us wanted it. Grief is the price of love, and love tells me to live. A life lived is a precious thing. Why then, I ask, does it seem that grief feels stronger than love? Every time I think about this, the world that I knew inside myself crashes. It's time for me to grow and embrace the life I knew, Jordan's life, my world. I know nothing could ever bring him back. I can choose to be happy and joyful about the fact that I knew and gave life to him and he was here.

My life is hinged between Jordan's death and the belief that I have that I will see him again. I made that statement to my sister just hours after getting the news of his death. I'm not sure if I said it for my benefit or hers. For some reason, I felt some sense of reassurance by saying it. I believed it at the time and still do. I think back to that day, and as we were standing there on the porch, that was the first thing I could think of saying, after the initial shock, of course. The onslaught of raw pain and grief came in the following days, weeks, and months. I went home to Washington to be alone with my thoughts after my brother showed me a picture of a newly erected cross in the spot where my son had just died on. I sat through a long painful cold winter. I cried every day, and this is when I realized I truly was lost. Sadness was my best friend. I couldn't get away from myself, and no road was long enough to drive to leave it behind or outrun it. Reminding myself every day that my child was dead seemed more painful than the time I was first told. It was like a hot poker stabbing me in the heart every time my mind would run across that thought. The scar is so big, I feel unrecognizable. People know me though. I'm still here. I thought I would just crumble and die from the weight of grief. I was hanging onto Jordan as if he were still here, still alive. My precious boy was no longer living, and I knew I had to let him go if I was ever to crawl up from the depths of this storm that gripped me. I had to release him from my aching heart if I ever was to move on. I held on to those words I said on that porch months earlier when I learned of his passing, and I felt comfort. It gave me something to look forward to at the end of my life. I had to do this for myself. With all the courage and leftover love and my broken heart, I gathered up a bunch of pictures of my beautiful boy and went to see my pastor. I told him that I had to let him go, and I knew he understood what I meant. My wounded, aching heart was broken and bleeding. The day was February 3, 2009, exactly three months from the day of Jordan's passing. The pastor and I went into his office and talked for a few minutes, and then he prayed for what seemed an eternity. I felt at ease as he prayed. I felt a sense of release, a calmness afterward, and the words, "I will see him again," echoed through my mind once again. When I let him go, I gave him back to God. I thanked him for letting me have this precious soul for the short time I did and for letting me be his mommy. My heart is broken, but I had the honor of raising the most beautiful child. I called him mine until God called him home. This is still so unreal as I write this, but this is my reality. I will see him again. This is what I hang onto to this day. Grass grows in winter, and I know I will get through this because God said I would. I will always be grateful for the time my pastor took to be with me, those few minutes that seemed like hours. They will last a lifetime that I will never forget. Thank you, Kevin Gerchak.

I still carry with me the deep sadness. It's a little softer now, but if I don't stay busy, I know I will fall into a million useless pieces. I keep my faith and try to walk a straight line and live a good life because I want to see my boy again. When I think about it, those three words, *let him go*, I think of dread. I feel like it's one of those times that was beyond the point of no return. Once it's done, it's done. I don't regret it, don't get me wrong. I know it was the right thing to do for me. It's what I had to do. I cannot go back to something that's not there, so I must move forward to the life that is waiting for me. I must look to the future and know that I will survive this. It's all that's left for me. I have no choice.

People say what doesn't kill you makes you stronger. One thing I'm sure of, they weren't talking about child loss. I'm positive that's not what they had in mind coining this phrase. I don't really know if anyone knows what they meant. Maybe they meant that if you were doing something really stupid and you didn't die, you were smarter to not do it again. At any rate, they weren't focused on the death of a child when this phrase came into existence, but it brings up a good point to me in my life. Losing my child, however life-altering and tragic it has been, has made me stronger, stronger in the sense that nothing can hurt me now that I have been through the worst thing anyone can go through. I now know that I can do anything, and there's nothing that will hurt me like this has. Time is my witness, and I am stronger now, emotionally and mentally. I have had to adapt. I have overcome.

I have no excuse for not getting things done in my life. I have the greatest reason there can be for moving on and living. Nothing should stand in my way. Through the most inhospitable season of my life, I grew. Look at your life, and consider all the things you have been through and have accomplished. There's something inside of you that pushes you on to survive. I live for my child, who is not here physically, but he is all around me in memory. That's my reason. I don't speak for everyone as we're not the same, you and me, but live for your child and what they have inspired in you. Keep their memories alive. Remind people they were here, and tell the great stories of their lives. You have been made strong through the loss of your child. You can now endure anything that comes your way. I know there are tears and sadness and tremendous heartbreak, but, dear one, you are a survivor. You are here for a reason. I know you are broken and bleeding and you may not want to hear these words because, deep down, you want to stay where you're at, where your child is. I was there too. I didn't want anyone to tell me I was going to be okay. Did they walk in my shoes? With the gentle breezes of time washing over you and the kindness you give to yourself, changes of healing will come.

Anger Has No Home

A nger. It's a coarse word—a very hostile emotion. It can take us over like wildfire out of control until all we see or feel is red. Our lives can become completely controlled by it. It can dictate our every word, and at times, it just becomes too heavy to bear. Soon, we carry it around like a friend, one we've grown accustomed to having around and begin to know very personally. Anger can feel like a noose tied to your neck, and it grows tighter with every thought. In my own life, anger, as I have come to realize, is futile. When I think of Jordan's death and all the whys and how come, my thoughts turn to anger, only second, at times, to sadness. I no longer want anger to have a place to turn to in my heart. It has grown too heavy and ugly. I no longer want this to be the first thought that enters my mind when I wake. I want to be the one who dictates how I think and feel and not the anger lurking in the back of my mind. I am fully aware of its presence. It is from learning on my own and choosing how I will feel that has made a world of difference in my life. I have become tolerant of anger and do not let it have the power over me to crush my spirits. After all, anger is a dead-end road.

It leads nowhere. I now get off that road as quickly as I can because I do not want to walk through life filled with bitterness and anger. It gets me nowhere. We may think it makes us feel better that somehow we are justified in what has happened to us. My heart longs for a soft place to fall and be done with anger and the torment it brings.

I have, silently and lovingly, lived out silent, imaginary experiences in my mind that will never come to fruition since Jordan's death. I know there are things that will never happen for and with him. He will never get married or have children of his own. He'll never fulfill the dream of the career he set his sights and heart on. There are too many "nevers" to count. I am sure any bereaved parent can relate to this. These events and others that will never take place are more than enough to enrage any parent to no end. All these things that won't happen affect me in my life. For the sake of dwelling on them and keeping sane, I have learned to live with this fact. Just knowing he won't be stopping by the house later or knowing he isn't going to call to say, "I love you, Mommy," fills my heart with anguish. Learning to live with his death alone is an ordeal. Topping it off with the what-ifs, whys, and "why him" compounds the pain tenfold.

I have let my anger go. It's not a part of me any-more. I realize it's impossible to be completely free of it, but deep down, this is not how I want to live anymore. I know in my heart that my son wouldn't want this either.

For each parent who has lost a child, I'm certain, some dreams came true while their child walked this earth, but for others, sadly, did not. Even though this may be the case, our hearts and futures were shattered when our child left this earth. The pain of one person's loss of a child is no greater or less than that of another's. I pray we all find our own peace through this hostile jungle and discover for ourselves the things that carry us through it.

The Last Goodbye

When Jordan died, my eyes were opened to a whole new kind of love, a love I had never realized existed until that moment. It was like loving him for the first time. The love I thought I had and felt for my baby—that love exploded. It awoke in me like something I never knew could be more than what it was. It became deeper and more meaningful than anything I had ever experienced before. It was like I never really loved him but said I did, and yes, I felt it, but now, that love was in full bloom. I truly realize now the full emotional meaning of the love for a child, our child, after he or she passes away. All our hopes and dreams pass away with them, but the love just grows because of that, and the memories are all that's left. It keeps getting stronger. What the heart wants eats away at us, and there is no going back. We've told our child "I love you" more times than we can count or remember. My heart is overflowing with the need to express that love. That leftover love that has nowhere to go— leftover love—that's the only thing I can come up with to describe it. It's there, and it's big, and it needs to be expressed. It's not extra. It just can't be given to the rightful recipient, the one it was made for. What do we do with the leftover love we are full of?

I won't be seeing Jordan again on this earth. My thoughts ramble, and I wish for more time with him. I wasn't ready for him to go. Would I ever have been? I wish for more talks, more hugs, more time, more life. With every passing day I don't see him, I just want him back more. Thoughts of the future that could have sparked anger inside of me. I miss him terribly. I've been told it gets easier, but seriously, don't ever let anyone tell you that. Period. Don't listen to that! If there is anyone who can say this to you, they have never walked in your shoes. Do not give anyone the power to dictate to you how you should feel. Only you can decide your feelings for yourself. I have said it gets harder because I am no longer in shock, and I have become more aware of the situation, more aware of his death, myself, and my feelings. My thoughts, at times, maybe unorganized, but still, it's not any easier to comprehend that my child is dead. Within myself, I have learned to cope with it better, and still, the love grows stronger. The love has smoothed out some of the rough edges, and I now embrace the fact that I had Jordan for the time that I did. There is no alternative. I want to move on and be happy for his sake. There is no fiercer love than that love of a mother for a child, and there is nowhere for it to go.

Love means never having to say goodbye. It seems to be true. Since love in relationships has already been established, there's no need for a goodbye. Love is the foundation of them. I am guessing that there is a great percentage of parents who never got to say goodbye to their child. It's just one of the many things that eat away at us—a regret. Please give yourself a break! You are a loving, caring parent, and you did not know what the future held for you or your child. I may not be using the most sensitive words here, but none of us can tell the future. We can't see into it. None of us know what will happen tomorrow or the next day or the next five minutes. I think back on the day of Jordan's passing, November 3, 2008, of all the things to be doing; that day, the day he died, I was gathering up his baby clothes out of a small, rundown shack that had been stored in a shed in my sister's yard years earlier. I finally got around to this task and wanted to take them back home with me to Washington. I had been over to Idaho for a visit with family. Jordan was also living there at the time. I was in the backyard going through these clothes when Jordan showed up with a couple of (girl) friends. We visited and talked for a while, and I was so grateful to be seeing him. Before they left to continue on their day, he came to me and wrapped me in a big bear hug and said, "I love you, Mommy."

I answered back, "I love you too, Jory."

The hug was a long one, and it seemed as though he would never let me go. I can still remember that warm, loving embrace, the last one. It felt like the ending of something when he did let me go. Jordan truly gave excellent hugs, bear hugs. I can still feel the embrace and the love he showed for me that day, that minute. That was the last we saw of each other. Those were the last words we ever spoke to one another. My heart aches now for that again, for what it can't have.

Jordan went on his way with his friends, and I finished up with the baby clothes and then went to my mother's house a few miles away. It was around 7:00 p.m. as we were eating dinner when a police cruiser showed up at the house. They were there to deliver the horrible, life-changing news that Jordan had been in an accident and that he didn't make it— DIDN'T MAKE IT!—the most horrible news that shattered my life into pieces. I instantly fell to my knees there on the porch where I stood. I began slamming my fists down again and again onto the floor screaming, "NO, NO, NO. NOT MY JORDAN!" There are no words to explain how I felt at that very moment. Jordan's life was over. The book was shut. The switch turned off. His life played in my mind like a movie that wasn't real, but it was. He was here, and now he was gone, and the movie was over. It is the end of this story because there are no do-overs. I have no words to describe the feeling of complete emptiness of living without my son that has enveloped me since his passing. I am stuck on this day.

Today, my heart is broken into a million pieces. My life is undone. Pieces missing. How do I go on dealing with everything out of place? How do I live? How am I going to make it through this without my Jordan? These are just some of the questions. These are just a few of the thoughts I have asked myself over the years. These things, at times, plague my mind, heart, and soul. In the early days when this pain was so raw, so fresh, uncovered, and bare for the whole world to see, survival seemed out of reach. For one moment, it seemed like the world knew for one second that my child died and then it forgot. I felt left behind to grieve, and everybody else just went on about its business. Life moved on, and I was at a standstill. For fourteen years, I felt like I wasn't moving at all.

No parent should ever have to say goodbye to their child. I pray the last time you saw your child it was with love and the time you spent with him or her was memorable. I pray this was the case with you and not one of regret. Regret is a horrible thing, a thing that can stalk you and hang around and torment you for years on end, for a lifetime. I can only wish you are not carrying this around.

The love I have for my son is great and at times heavy. It has nowhere to go and longs to be released. This is a burden I am happy to carry. This keeps me alive. The grief, however, is a burning, searing pain that cuts like a knife. There is no road long enough that I can drive on to wear out this grief and no mountain high enough that it cannot follow me. No ocean can take it out with the next tide. It will be with me till the day I die. On that day, I believe I will see my son again, and my heart will cry no more, and I will no longer be broken.

It has been nearly fifteen years since Jordan has been gone. Because of his death, a new normal has come to me in which to live in. My life has changed, and so I have adapted to those changes. Grass grows in winter, and so I must. I have grown through these changes, although it seems they were invisible along the way to the eye. During the harshest time of my life, I have prevailed.

Love means never having to say goodbye. I'm sure we've all heard that before. It probably has different meanings to us all. A good number of us know the outcome of that saying. Some of us—okay, most of us—never got to say goodbye. It's heart-wrenching when a child breathes his last breath, and we weren't there for it. I am speculating here, but I think, to MOST parents, that not being able to say goodbye haunts them. I don't know if I would have ever said it because I wouldn't have wanted him to leave, to die, had I known. I did tell my son goodbye. How was I to know it was the last one? How was I to know I would never see him again? How was I to know, at that very moment, that destiny was happening? At that very moment in time, that's what was happening. None of us know if our child is going to die, and we don't have a crystal ball, but personally, to me, goodbyes are sad to the very soul.

The Memory Box

A few days after Jordan was killed, one of my brothers who had been out to the crash site showed me a picture he had taken on his phone. It was of a cross on the side of the road. That cross had been put up in the very spot where Jordan died, and that broke me. It was too soon to see something like that. To me, that meant finality. I barely had time to process the information I had about his passing and, now, this. He really was dead, or there wouldn't have been a cross on the side of the road where he had the accident. It hit me hard with horrendous force that my son, my only child, was really dead. That particular memory haunts me. I immediately said that I wanted to go home, to be alone with my thoughts. I wanted to go back home to Washington, where I could wallow in my pain and grief and whatever else it had in store for me.

Not long after getting home, I started in on my house. I looked around at all the stuff there, things taking up space that I knew I wasn't ever going to need or use. I barely had time to adjust to Jordan's passing, and I was faced with what was to become the second of many adjustments to come—clear-

25

ing out the stuff, the material things I no longer needed. None of these things mattered anymore. I couldn't share anything with Jordan anymore. I felt an enormous sense of guilt for having these things, these stuff, these stupid, useless junk. I also felt guilty about eating and anything else I did, for that matter. I felt because Jordan couldn't, and I thought I should stop doing all the things that brought me joy. These things now brought me guilt because he was gone. I know this makes little sense, but walk with me here. I still don't understand it. Anyway, I remember walking through my house and wanting to get rid of things. I was mad at myself for having these things. Maybe in this moment I felt my life was over. Maybe this was a way of my mind coping, lashing out. My child gave me a deep sense of life, of living, and when he died, that went with him.

I used to save and collect a lot of stuff, simple things like knick-knacks, books, etc. I always thought that someday I am going to need that or this. I think there's a little bit of a hoarder in all of us. Some maybe more than others, who knows. I'm not one to judge. In the end, we all know it's just going to sit there up on that shelf and collect dust.

Today, I keep and collect things but to a minimum. I still feel the guilt every time I bring a treasure home though. I feel the sadness from all those years ago and how Jordan isn't here to listen to my story about how I acquired it. To not be able to share this with him is pure emptiness. At times, I just have to tell myself I don't need that thing and drive right on by the second-hand store. After all, I can't take it with me. Today, I keep more things in my memories than I do on a shelf. They don't get lost, and they don't gather dust. Some days, I survive on those memories, and there's not a single thing wrong with accumulating them. There's not anything wrong with accumulating material things either, so long as you have a place to put them. After all, we may need that ole blue torn lampshade with the tassels hanging off the bottom and that ghastly crack down the side, someday, maybe, just someday. If you ever find a lamp and you need shade, there ya go. Voila! You've got a new lamp, with memories.

In all seriousness, there are of course things we keep for real memories' sake: precious things, like pictures, newspaper clippings, gifts from loved ones, and little things made by small loving hands of our child in those early school years. These are things they may have drawn or painted, things that have been glued or stapled together to create a magical work of art, things they gave to us out of their love for us. A scribbled-on piece of paper or a colored paper from a book to me is something to cherish. These are the things that keep the holes plugged up in our memory box in our mind. For some, there is empty space in the memory box. It was designed to hold a lifetime and yet was cut short. The spaces belong to the things I did not keep and for the life that wasn't finished. I remember a few things I did not keep and now wonder why I did not. I feel like kicking myself. Who would have known I was going to need that to keep my sanity or to look at in later years, like now and relive the memory of it? I need it now. At times I worry and get anxious and wish for that one thing back to complete the box. In the end, none of us knew what the future held, so we lived our lives not knowing that tomorrow would be the last day to add to the memory box. For that one thing we threw away, we will pine away, wishing we could get it back. We just want to hold it and look at it one last time. So, parents, hold onto that colored picture or that favorite toy. These things may be the only thing you have to keep your sanity with one day. You may need it to complete you or your memory box.

Some things I'm sure everyone has saved are pictures of their child, looking back and comparing photos and seeing how far he or she has come and grown. These are lasting memories. Please burn them into your heart and mind! These are the things that satisfy the heart, somewhat when you feel yourself losing all touch with reality and think you will go insane because your child is not coming home. You need this to hold onto. In life or death, these moments can add life to your memory box.

Save all those small things just because. Pull them out now, and then and look at them. Your children are your flesh and blood, and these things help you to stay connected to who they are. Children are to be loved. Cherish them. Keep your memory box full.

I have quite a few things that were my son's. Most of the items have a story to tell that I keep safely tucked away in my memory box. I take them out now and again to relive the good times or the story behind the memory, to feel close to Jordan again. Sometimes, these things bring a smile and other times a tear. Either way, they are mine and a blessing now that he's gone.

I spent a lot of time with Jordan when he was small and very young. Reading to him and teaching the alphabet and numbers to him is a very strong memory of mine. By the time he was three, he could write the ABCs and write numbers one through ten. I was a proud mama. I kept the paper he first wrote those letters and numbers on. I have it stashed away somewhere. What means the most to me now is the memory of it. I may find it someday. That would be a gem to hold again in my hands. I can see it in my mind still. I remember each little line and number made by his tiny hand. That piece of paper is a huge addition to my memory box. It's a keeper.

Gaping Holes and
Empty Chairs

As each holiday, birthday, or family gathering comes and goes each year, I think of how wrong it is that Jordan is never in attendance. I feel selfish and think it's extremely unfair! I replay in my mind, backward, down through the years, even to his birth, all those events he was in attendance. I dig way back deep into the files of my memories and quickly watch everyone. My, the times we had. Life seemed so perfect back then. Maybe perfect isn't the word to describe it—content, maybe. All was good in our world. All the chairs were filled during "normal" times in our lives. This is living a new normal. I look around at family members and see who is there and think of how unfair it is that everyone has their own personal, special people they call their own there, who belong to them. I don't have anyone here that belongs to me. Self-pity sits by my side. Sooner or later, I think, why me? Why Jordan? My mind gets violently ripped away from what's really going on, and I wallow silently in my own torn world. It seems no one else cares that he's not here, but I know that's not true. We all have our lives to live. It's the grief and pain speaking to me, telling me how to think and feel and this is only natural. This is the course of grief. I wish for Jordan to be everywhere I look and go. I wish for him to be at every family and holiday gathering. It's been nearly fourteen years, and I've learned that this feeling will most likely be with me till the day I die. Jealousy or envy would probably be a better word that describes the feelings I get rather than self-pity. I don't feel sorry altogether for myself that he's not sitting there in that chair; it's more like, "Why can't he be there? Why did it have to be him?" It's more of an envious feeling because others have what I do not. This, in return, makes me feel so alone, singled out in a way. Everyone has their children and their children's children, and I have no one. I am a single person, a single mother with no one to call her own. At times, I feel left out and forgotten, left behind. I'm on my own now. This surely sounds like self-pity now. Ha-ha. But I know better. I need to pick myself right back up off the floor and stop wallowing. I know that I am loved and that others loved Jordan. I also know these are not the feelings to be having on the road to healing, whatever that may be. It's not self-pity. I have felt more sorrowful for Jordan than for myself, sorrow that he is gone, sorrow that he cannot be here and experience life as we knew it. I describe it as a moment of remembrance and reflection of the past and what it once held for me. I believe it still has significance, and somehow that can't really be prevented from happening. I am strong at heart, but these things are going to happen no matter what. After all, I am only human trying to navigate this thing called grief.

Plastic Flowers

B e it real or fake, flowers can grace most anything, inside or out. Our surroundings seem to come to life with vivid, colorful flowers of any kind. Whether on a vintage wooden wishing well or a trellis over a walkway, flowers of any kind can dress up your life. Flowers come in many colors, sizes, shapes, and varieties. When choosing them, we are most likely drawn to the color first; second, the type; and lastly, the size. Of course, plastic flowers last the longest as opposed to real ones.

The home I once lived in had a long rectangular porch, as most porches are, I suppose. There were long wooden planks on the floor, and an overhang from the side of the house to the edge was about eight feet. The planked flooring gave the porch a rustic look I adored. I adorned the porch with two large wicker chairs that sat in a corner, and a small table between the two gave it a great personality. Every year I would gather up at least fifteen pots of various shapes and sizes and attach hangers to some. I spent around $50.00 or so on annuals and potting soil and just went crazy potting those beautiful flowers knowing by the end of a month or so, they would all be filled out and blossoms would fill the pots. I knew they would be gorgeous. I placed them around the porch and hung many up.

I worked a full-time job and a part-time job while raising a wonderful son, which kept me busy. There came a year when I felt I just didn't have the time to fill all those pots. I wanted flowers, though, so I came up with a solution. I still wanted beauty but didn't want to do all the work. Beautiful colors and dancing flowers were still my goals. My solution is plastic flowers, although they didn't dance like real ones. On a day off from work, I made the time to visit second-hand stores in the area. I gathered up and bought all the fake flowers I could find. I ended up spending about $10.00 for all my treasures, which is a far cry from the cost of real flowers. I was excited to take them home and create my masterpieces. I joyfully took on the task of filling each pot. I carefully placed a variety of colors and shapes and types into each one. It was great. Now, not only do I have flowers on my porch, but I had them year-round, all for a fraction of the cost. Throughout all the seasons, spring, summer, fall, and winter, they remained. No one could tell they weren't real. They were timeless.

We all know plastic flowers aren't real, and yet they are a beautiful thing to look at and enjoy. Their beauty can be held in the eye of the seeker looking for a little joy in their life. Like us, first impressions are taken from what we see on the outside. I sometimes feel I have something in common with those plastic flowers. Yes, sometimes, I feel like a plastic flower. As a grieving mother, I hide what's on the inside. The outside is what others see first. There is also beauty on the inside. It is just too painful to show it at times. Sometimes, I get overwhelmed by the pain. I guess what I'm trying to say here is that we hide behind beauty and don't let others see what's really on the inside, the beauty that's there. Many don't know what's behind the beauty, the tears, sadness, and turmoil that's going on inside. Trying to portray to others that things are fine as we go about our day can wear us down. Grief will never go away when it comes to such a loss as this. We go on living a new normal life. Nothing is the same for us anymore, and sometimes, I feel like that plastic flower that shows no emotion, sheds no tears but shows beauty on the outside.

Pieces of Me

Sometimes, I often wonder what life would be like living on a paved road. Most of our lives are spent living on rough, rocky dirt roads, while our hearts and bodies are getting jostled around to and fro as we deal with what life has to offer up. There were many rocky roads I journeyed down, not knowing where they would lead me. Life is mostly trial and error, and we sure learn the fast hard way what works and what doesn't. It seems, though, I always knew which road to take, that is, until Jordan died. At least, it seemed that way. All roads since then have been hit or miss as far as knowing what to do with my life. A new future must be written. The one I realized, the one I had in mind, shattered and fell away like dead leaves fall from a tree in winter, never to be again. I became so lost after Jordan died and felt so alone that everything was just like a blank page. My road was very rocky. There was nothing written anymore as far as I was concerned. The story didn't end the way I had imagined. It doesn't matter how long I sit and stare at the story. There are no pages to fill it. Jordan was my future as well as my past and present. It is all clear to me now. We live for our children, whether it's for their life or for their death. Our very existence revolves around them. There's no denying that our every waking moment, every breath we take, is consumed by them, and there's not a single thing we do without them on our minds. My life is now consumed by the death of my son. This thought never leaves my mind. It is there in every single thing I do and say. His death is literally there with every beat of my heart. When he was alive, that gave me a purpose to live. He was my child. He was my flesh and blood, my reason to live. I cannot imagine one single parent not feeling this way. It isn't possible. Anyone who has lost a child to death cannot truthfully say that they don't literally feel like a living, breathing piece of them is missing. You feel incomplete. My child made me completely content. His life, his existence, made mine. I physically, mentally, and emotionally feel incomplete. This pain we feel is real. It is hell to go through, and some days, we feel we can't go another day. We lived for our children when they were alive, and ultimately, I have learned we live for them through their death. I am a firm believer that if I ever want to see Jordan again, and I will, I must stay here. No matter how broken I am, it is not my place to take my own life. Only the giver of life is the taker. So my life goes on because of him.

It is impossible to forget that Jordan died, and a new normal must be lived and created. I have learned over the years not to give power over to the unwanted thoughts that plague my mind. I have stepped into my new normal, it seems, some time back, and has grown with it. I never learned how to deal with death and the impact it has on a person. Each one of us is different, and we all learn what works best for us in our own lives and in our own time. It's a slow process to get to where you need to be. A place where you feel good about life again is the goal. I have lost loved ones in my lifetime, but for me, personally, none has been as devastating to the very core of my soul or life-changing as the death of my own child. It is hard to say this without sounding like I am belittling the death of one compared to another; this is not my intention. I just know that the loss of a child feels like losing yourself. It's like your whole world, and you don't want to go on anymore. You don't want to live another day without them. You just want to lay down and die just to be with your child. It's impossible to believe they are dead. You fight these feelings within yourself and lose the battle every time. You ask, and ask, and ask, and never get any answers to your questions. They simply don't exist. You are totally lost and completely broken to pieces. You don't even know how to think anymore. Your mind is just not letting this in. I know I am not alone when I say these things. That is some comfort. The single most horrifying experience a parent can go through is the death of a child. Nothing else in this lifetime can even come close to touching or hurting us this deep. For days, even weeks, or months, we float through life, trying to take in the unbelievable as if it was a dream or a trance. We try to figure out if it really happened. For me, most of the time afterward, I was alone. I tried desperately to keep in touch with reality, as if I knew what that was anymore. I was alone; I knew that. Bringing up the past and recalling those first few months when my pain was so raw, like an open wound that would burst open the second someone looked at me, is like baring my all, my soul, wide open for the whole world to see. It's like reading a book that's so sad and that can never be rewritten. The end is the same for this lifetime. Again, the what-ifs come to mind, and I stop and go over them all once again. I don't suppose I'll ever stop thinking about them because there is that part of me that thinks, *Maybe there was something that I could have done to prevent his death.* Deep down in the core of my being, I know there wasn't. I am human, after all. As a mother, I instinctively welcome futile thoughts and ideas to turn back time. Of course, it is not possible, and I reluctantly tell myself it's over and there's nothing I could have done. Sadness sets in again. I am forced, ultimately, to remember and face the cold fact that, indeed, Jordan is dead, and no time spent begging the clock to bring him back will work.

Seeking a new normal after child loss is what every parent gently evolves into. I guess we don't really look for it; rather, it looks for us. This new thing gradually falls into place and takes over. It's kind of like something we step into without really knowing. As we try to live our day-to-day, shattered life, changes can be subtle, but they do take place about and within us as we grieve. We may not even notice the milestones as they take place. Certain aspects of our lives become automatic because of sadness or guilt that has taken over. One day, you will be doing something or talking with a friend and catch yourself laughing and having a good time. The next moment, you realize what just happened and discover that you have made progress. The guilt comes after that, but you must stay strong. Don't let the guilt take you backward. You have grown. It's not about forgetting. It's about growing through the winter.

Normally, I am not around a lot of people, except at work. Here, I wear the biggest mask there is. Because of this, I would say for myself that no one has really seen a lot of the changes I have gone through. In a way, this sounds like no one ever really knew me, the real me. However, I know me, and I know my heart and the way I used to be. If anyone has seen changes in me, they have not mentioned them. I wonder if this is the same for everyone. In the end, I do believe we change and become more aware of our surroundings. We pay more attention to things now. The small things, the little things matter more to me now. I find myself caring more and having more compassion for others than I had in the past. I know how quickly life can disappear. It only takes a second. My thoughts and feelings for others are stronger and more meaningful now.

I cannot retrace my steps down through the last fourteen years I have lived without my child in my life and, therefore, cannot pinpoint each change I have gone through, but I can glance at myself and see who that person was then and who she is now. I could write a book. I have grown through all those terrible winters of my life and have found some sun. There is a peace in me now. I don't cry every day. There are many times when the waves of sadness try to bring me to my knees and surrender all that I am to grief, to the ugly fact that I was reminded of, once again, that my Jordan has died. This is hard. This is brokenness. I pick myself up now that I have been slapped in the face again by grief. I will not forget. The pain I feel when I think of him is still there and as blunt as day one. This never goes away. I push through these feelings and become stronger and can stand longer. Am I out of tears? Has my heart grown callous? Though I have cried many days in the past, it's like reliving his death for the first time. I am ready for it. I must go on. Life does go on, and I know none of us to want one more person to say that to us. I used to say every day that this grieving is like one long, ghastly day that never seems to end. Someday, it will. For now, the new normal I have cautiously let in will live.

My mind now takes me to the things in life I don't want to miss out on, things like beautiful sunsets or sunrises. No two are alike. They speak to me of a solid promise of a new day, each in its own way, a day that will be better than the one before. Like a sunrise or sunset, the colors of life erupt joyfully, with magnificence only they can hold. I surely don't get to see each one, but I try because if I miss one, there's no going back. It's gone forever. It's a memory to behold. It's like filling in that blank space of a new beginning, and I can write it any way I want. It gives me hope to strive for a better day, it pushes me to go on, and I grow with it.

Wishes in Stone

Unfold my ashes on Shefoot Mountain
For that's where I long to be
And I will rise on a zephyr like the wings of an eagle
And he will peer down upon me
I will gently light on creation below
Make it my abode for evermore
Blossoms will glow in my stead
And boughs of giants will shade my bed
Scatter my ashes on Shefoot Mountain
Don't weep or lament for me
Twilight won't steal my memory
For it's as strong as the wind
I'll be in the rain and in the snow
I will go with the seasons wherever they flow
The sun will warm and shine upon me
And the rivers will flow beside me
Mountains will rise and know I am there
And never will I have a troubling care
Spread my ashes on Shefoot Mountain
For that's where I long to be
There is peace and serenity waiting for me
It's as close as heaven can be

Eternal Memories

I 've got what seems to be a lifetime of memories of my sweet Jordan, and yet that life wasn't over. There's not enough paper to be found to write them all down and all my feelings about them. A million or more memories it seems, good and bad, happy and sad, but none that I will forget.

Many of the memories we made are of doing outdoor activities like fishing, camping, hunting, and hiking. We enjoyed doing a lot of things together with other family members and friends. So much fun was had by all. I wish these times were here again to experience them once more, but things change, and people grow and move on. Now, a new generation is hopefully doing all the great things we did all those years ago.

I took Jordan on a day hunting trip in the fall of one year. He was around eleven or twelve. On this trip, he shot his first grouse. Every young boy, I'm sure, is on cloud nine the moment they slay their first critter. He was so proud. I, too, was proud of him. I was so happy to be there with him for this "first." We were in the mountains of north Idaho, where every-one and anyone who hunts goes if they want to see wildlife or bag the big one. Together, Jordan and I went on more hunting trips but never bagged anything other than that little grouse.

Jordan grew to love the outdoors as much as I did and all those who live in the area.

Fishing was also a great sport for both of us, and we participated in it every chance we got. This is one activity Jordan took on abundantly into adulthood. He loved fishing more than hunting, I believed. There are many rivers and bodies of water in which to fish in north Idaho, too numerous to count. These lakes and rivers and are now open year-round in this area.

One fishing trip I remember well comes to mind that we went on. It's a great fish story. We were at a lake by the name of Killarney. The day was very cold and windy. The lake surface was choppy and dark, and if anything wasn't nailed down, it was being taken away with the next big gust. No one wanted to even stay on the docks with their poles and lines cast out. We were out fishing, on that blustery day, with an old family friend who has since then passed away. He is missed. Jordan must have been eight or nine at the time and was very eager to fish and loved every bit of this crappy weather just to fish. He took in every shred of knowledge our friend gave him about fishing and rigging the lines. Our goal today was a pike. We figured since the weather was quite chilly, we had a good chance of hooking some nice ones closer to shore where the water may be a bit warmer than further out in the deeper parts. We cast our lines out, sat in our cars, and waited. Around 1:00 p.m., just after we had eaten lunch and not paying too much attention to our bobbers, we glanced out at the lake beyond the docks for the movement of our bobbers. Mine hadn't moved at all, but when we looked for Jordan's, it wasn't where it should have been, and neither was his pole. Both were gone! We flew out of the car and ran down to the dock, searching for his pole. His balloon, which we used for a bobber, was about 150 feet or so out in the lake and slowly heading south. By this time, both of us were so excited we just stood there, not quite sure what to do next. I came up with an idea to reel my line in and then cast it out, not too far from the dock, to see if I could snag his line; not really knowing where it was, I had to try something. I cast out about ten feet into the general direction in which I thought his line and pole would have fallen in or, in this case, pulled in. I began to reel in my line, and luckily, I had snagged his line bringing up the pole. You never saw a happier little kid once he saw that pole and had it in his hands. He proceeded to reel in his line, fish on, and sure enough, he bagged a nice pike. It was only a two-footer, but to him, it was a trophy fish. This was his first pike, a great accomplishment for such a young man. He truly did have a big fish story about the one that didn't get away. As it turned out, he was the only one who caught any fish that day. Our fishing partner and I never lived that one down. This was truly a great trip and a story for the books.

I wish for more fishing and hunting trips with this precious boy. Sadly, I'll never stand alongside a riverbank or walk through forests again with Jordan making more memories. In the end, life goes on, the world keeps turning, and the clock keeps ticking. Gratefully, this memory is written in stone, as is the next.

As I mentioned earlier, there is an amazing abundance of things to do and see here in north Idaho. One special gem to me is a place called Shefoot Mountain. It is in the red Ives ranger district of Shoshone county. It is south of Wallace over a pass and through some magnificent country. The drive to this peak is simply phenomenal. Every mile driven to this beast of a mountain is well worth the twisty, turny, wash-boardy, dusty roads. The scenery alone will leave you breathless and cause you to want to never leave. The pass, Moon Pass, offers outstanding 360-degree views. The reward at the end was Shefoot Mountain. This trip always delivered what we went there for, and I wouldn't hesitate to go at every chance I got. Shefoot boasts of a 6,306 feet elevation, and it really feels as though you are standing on top of the world. This was a favorite place for us to go on a day trip while camping on the St. Joe River far below. Squaw creek campground or Loop Creek. We always stayed nearly a week, which never seemed long enough to take in all the beauty nature had to offer there. We fished, hiked, and took quick dips in the icy cold runoff of the St. Joe. I'll never forget a single memory made there, and I took them away with me. I had a full heart at the time. For many years, beginning when Jordan was around six, a friend and I would plan our yearly camping trips for the month of July. We camped at Squaw Creek for about four years in a row during this vacation time. We pulled a small camper down with us, so it wasn't really roughing it in the woods, but it made some things a lot easier. At least one day on each camping trip, we made a beautiful trip to the Shefoot Mountain. That one day we went was usually spent up there till sundown. We captured the most beautiful sunsets on camera and in our minds. These are the memories that will never fade with time.

My Jordan passed away in 2008, and since then, I have only made the trip once. The opportunity just hasn't come, or maybe since he can't go, I have lost the urge to be there. I see him there in my mind on top of that mountain, a little boy standing against the sunset. He's wearing blue jeans and a white T-shirt, blond curls covering his head and blue eyes smiling back at me. He's always the little boy so full of love and life. He's sitting on my knee, and he never grows up. This is how I always see him. He was the ultimate joy to me, a treasure to be around, and I never ever, not once, tired of him. Oh, how I wish I could turn back time.

In the summer of 2008, Jordan called me, as he often did, asking for directions to Shefoot. He and a cousin had wanted to make the trip up and weren't sure how to get there. He wanted to visit the place we took him to as a child and take in the beauty as an adult. I happily gave the directions. Twice they tried in the months to come, and twice they failed. They never made it to Shefoot, and I felt bad for them. I only wish I could have been there to help, to direct them or even tag along. The drive was just as adventurous as standing on top or hiking around the area and looking down over the cliffs to the valley below. The view is breathtaking. I was sad for him, knowing he never made it back there. Little did anyone know this would be the last summer of his life.

The following November, sadly, Jordan passed away. He will never again step out on a journey to stand on top of that or any other mountain with me or anyone else. Knowing how he tried to fulfill a dream twice and failed, I kind of got the feeling that was where he wanted to go to, to be. I took that to heart and planned on fulfilling that dream.

In 2010, two years after his passing, my pain and sorrow were still very fresh and raw to me, and I had it in my heart to carry out this last adventure with Jordan. I left my residence in Washington on September 3 and journeyed over to Idaho. I made a stop by Jordan's father's house because his ashes were still with him. They had been there since day 1. I wanted to get some to take with me on my trip. I was on a mission. To this day, Jordan's ashes are still resting on a shelf in his father's house. I have mixed feelings about this since I have nowhere to go to pay my respects. I have, however, felt comforted knowing he is safe. Even though I know he is no longer there in the body that he once was, I know where he is now, and that's what should give me comfort, but, in the end, he's not here in the flesh, and that gives me discomfort. I know where he is, although I'm not happy with it, but still, he is safe. As Jordan's ashes were gently and carefully being scooped from a plastic bag, I gave way to tears and sadness once again. I cried the whole time. Just thinking that these ashes were once my son's body broke me. I had with me a small brass container in which to put them in. I had picked it out and brought it with me, and it had always had a special meaning to me, and now it had a deeper meaning. It was now holding tiny pieces of my child. Dust—this was all that was left of him and his wonderful life, the only one of him in creation. I closed the lid on the ashes and cried some more. Just the thought and sight of my child in that form, ashes in a plastic bag, the reality of it all, broke my heart all over again. Any healing that had taken place in my heart in the previous two years up to this moment had been split wide open, and now, the wound would have to begin to scab over and begin to heal again. I left there that day with pieces of my son in my hands, carrying him to one of his final resting places, to be where he wanted to be.

September 4 was a beautiful sunny day. I set out on my mission alone, just me and Jordan and a bag of Cheetos—our favorite. Everything went smoothly on the trip, and the closer I got to Shefoot, the more the memories came flooding into my mind. Part of me was sad. Part of me was reluctant to let him go again. I felt as though this was the very last chapter of a book, the very last line where it says the end. It's like reading a book and you don't want to know the end, so you put it off because once it's done, it's done. There's no going back. Part of me felt good to be fulfilling a dream for him. For me, it was like that last line of the book and closing it.

My trip was a calm one and was met with only one hitch in the road, you could say. I was about half a mile from the top, the last stretch of road. This stretch of road ran along a bank to the right and a cliff to the left. The road ahead of me lay heavy with huge rocks that had been deposited year after year with every snowfall and thaw in spring. Along with the runoff and gravity, more and more rocks were deposited on the road every year. The rocks were so many in number that they looked like a dried-up riverbed instead of a dusty mountain road. I stopped my rig when I came upon this spot, and the dilemma I had lying before me told me to be on the cautious side. I sat there for a minute or two, contemplating whether to veer to the left or right. The thought of turning around never crossed my mind. One side was clearly not easier than the other as the rocks were equally large on both sides of the road. I thought for another moment, *I did have new tires and a four-wheel drive*, so fear flew out the window as I put it in gear and slowly, gently crawled over all those rocks and continued. I was determined to reach the top. Within another twenty minutes or so of slow mindful driving, I reached the summit. Still, in my rig, sitting on top, the magnificent view did not fail to please the eyes. It had been just as I remembered it so many years ago.

Still sitting in my rig on the very top, the magnificent view did not fail to please the eye. In my thoughts, I went back to all those happy years, years when Jordan was just a small boy and we stood there on that mountain together. We had the time of our lives. Now, he was gone, yet here I was, with him. I thought of the picture that was taken of the two of us standing near the edge of the cliff. I pictured his face and skin, tanned from the cheerful summer sun. I remember the summer my best friend and her family joined us one year. I remembered that year, and snow still lay on the ground in spots in July. I remember just standing here. Our world was good.

I finally made it out of my vehicle and walked to the edge with Jordan in my hands. I stood there and relived the memory of him standing there with me one more time. I imagined I would be throwing a priceless treasure over a cliff, never to be retrieved. I would never get it back. I'll never forget that day. There was a slight breeze, and as I took off the lid of the small brass coffin, ashes began to swirl and spill out, the wind took them, and they gently lay down on the ground not far from where I stood. I tipped the container, and the wind once again took the ashes away from me. The wind took some down the cliff face as I tilted it more. Some blew away with the gentle wind as if taking them to another place, never to return. He is there. I whispered a prayer as the ashes scattered about where they would, and I felt a sense about me that a promise had been fulfilled. Letting Jordan go that way, to me, was also a way of saying that, tragically, this really happened and life goes on. It didn't stop when he died, and it did not stop this day. After all these years, I still miss my son extremely. I miss everything about him and all there was to know about him. I know that life must go on. I must live on and be a productive member of society. I have no choice. I have this memory and many, many more of life with my child. I will never fish or hunt with him again. I will never again stand on top of a majestic mountain with him or look at his beautiful face. I will, however, see him again someday. Because of him, my life goes on. I have grown because of him. I have lived because of him.

A Million Useless Pieces

It is a scary thing to fall apart and lose the sense of who you are. Child loss can do this to you. Some circumstances in our lives require so much of our attention. Sooner rather than later, that's all we think about no matter what we do to distract our minds. Nothing works. The death of a beloved child can take your mind to places you don't want to go or thought you'd never be. If I let my mind take control of me, if I don't stay busy, I know I would fall into a million useless pieces. Today, this is where I am at. I'm trying to stay up and busy and not become a million useless pieces.

The Progress of Moving On

The deep sadness that has partnered up with me in my own life has truly worn out its welcome. I've concluded that there is more to life than being sad all the time. I realize what I'm going through is rough, but there is more to me than this. I know the grieving process will always be taking place within me, but when do I say stop? When do I say I don't want to feel like this anymore? This is a heavy burden to carry, but it doesn't always have to be this way. Moving on and being happy sometimes feels like a betrayal to our feelings or to our child. It's as if we are destined to be sad forever. Our children and their memories will never be forgotten, not by us or by any of the people who knew and loved them. I take pride in the stories others tell me about Jordan. I say, "Yep, that was my son!" The feeling I get from that is comforting and uplifting. I know that he touched someone else's life. As fate would have it, he's not here, but he knows, and oh, how I wish to God that he was here. His memory grows like grass grows in winter. They will live on in our hearts forever. This is what's left of him now, and I embrace that. I know I will see him again happy, healthy, and whole.

Using my pain as my purpose, I have tried to help others who are going through child loss. I have reached out to other moms just after hearing the sad news that they lost a child. Some of these women I knew already, and some are now friends. After learning of their own personal tragedy, my heart went out to them, and I had to meet up right away. I thought about what they must be going through and are going to go through in the days and months to come. I felt an overwhelming sense that I must go to comfort them in some small way. The sleepless nights and crying where the tears never end, they, too, must now endure. My heart bleeds for them. I gave my full attention and thought to their burden at this moment and not my own. No parent should have to go through this alone. I know all these moms now and will keep them in my thoughts and prayers. I pray they are doing well. When two of my closest friends, each, lost a grown child, I never dreamed it could happen so close to home to two of my dearest friends. I treasure these women. My heart broke for them and for the horrible, agonizing pain of grief they both would be enduring for years to come. My heart knows their hearts, and I wish there was a way to make them feel at peace, to ease their pain. Knowing how my heart feels and everything that surrounds it because of the loss of my child and now, they must also begin their journey of finding themselves all over again. I am tied to these girls by old friendships from the past and, ultimately, a new one because of the death of our children. I will always be here for them should they need me.

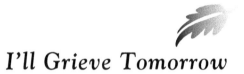

I'll Grieve Tomorrow

There is no statute of limitations for grief. It's not written in the stars or any book the length of time one should grieve. I know it takes time and, for some, longer than others. Grief will never stop. The fact that a tragedy occurred never goes away, and it seems it takes forever for your head and heart to acknowledge it. What everyone understands for himself as the definition of grief to be is not necessarily the same for everyone. We grieve and go through the motions, the process, according to who we are and how our lives have been impacted by the tragedy we have experienced. As the reality of that experience settles into our minds and we fully understand what has taken place, the grieving process begins. This is the natural way grieving is supposed to take place, I believe. Let it come. In my own life, I did just the opposite.

A day or two after Jordan's passing, I began the three-hundred-mile trip back home to Washington. I cried nearly the whole way while driving. The trip was just a long tearful blur. The next three months I spent mostly at home and still in shock, and the raw pain poured out of me constantly. I was a wreck. My mind was stuck on hold, and this could not possibly be true.

In February 2009, I found a job, three months after Jordan's passing. The relationship I was in at the time was extremely one-sided, and my partner was quite possibly the most selfish, needy person on the planet. Whatever the case, everything was always about him. He once told me, "You know, it's not like you are the only person who has ever lost anyone." This told me that not only did he not care but also that he didn't have the capacity in his brain to begin to understand the pain I was going through. His words were all for himself. He managed to twist the knife a little more with every un-caring action and hurtful word. This is when I knew I had to leave there. Over the next two years, he became a lying, cheating, manipulating man. He was a truck driver, which meant he was not home daily, but this also gave him endless opportunities for multiple affairs, which he blatantly denied and then pleaded for mercy after admitting they were true. After a few violent incidences on his part and emotional and mental abuse of me, I was afraid to leave. During these two years, as I was putting up with all the BS, I told myself, "I'll grieve tomorrow." I had to keep my sanity and deal with the jerk face and work my job. I cried every day but felt I had to hide my emotions because I was literally alone in this world and there certainly wasn't anyone around me who seemed to care. This man would ask me why I was crying. Really!

In February 2011, I planned to leave. I gave notice at my place of employment, packed my things into storage, and left while he was out on the road. I felt this was the only way I could do it, as bad as it sounds. I didn't look back, and again, I found myself crying during this long trip, only in the opposite direction. I was going back home. I was harassed by him for a solid ten months afterward. Then it all finally stopped.

So I'll grieve tomorrow. I don't even know what that means anymore. I have always told myself I would set aside some time to go somewhere and grieve, someday. There's just something inside of me that's connected to Jordan, obviously, that's calling me somewhere, somewhere that I can just be, somewhere where there is just time, no work, no distractions of everyday life, just for a while, time for me to just sit and think and reflect on my life, of Jordan's life, and of our lives together, and pay my respects to his passing and say a prayer. Maybe this is my way of working through grief. Maybe this is something I needed. Maybe me sitting here writing this is an internal way for me to find some sort of closure. I just wanted once upon a time to be that person I was supposed to be back then when all this happened, but I had to be someone else, for someone else.

When most people pass away, their bodies are normally laid to rest in a grave or cremated and laid to rest or cremated and the ashes scattered. Jordan's body was cremated but has never been laid to rest anywhere. His ashes are in an urn at his father's house on a shelf. I always knew he was in a safe place even though he was no longer there and even though there was no grave to visit to pay my respects. My intentions had always been to lay him down, but his father didn't want to.

His father lived thirty miles from me, here in Idaho, and I felt a sense of comfort knowing he was near. One day, Jordan's father informed me that he would be moving, five hundred miles away. We had a deal about Jordan's ashes that he was going to give them to me and that he would never take them away from me if he ever moved away. Since Jordan passed away, we had become closer and had a good relationship. Sadly, he did move away and took Jordan's ashes with him. How could he do this! He told me he didn't have Jordan while he was growing up. Granted, Jordan lived primarily with me, but his father did see him. I ceased all communication with him because this truly hurt me deeply. Two and a half years passed by without either messaging or speaking to the other. Sadly, tragedy struck Jordan's father once more when his wife passed away. God rest her precious soul. He messaged me asking if I would like to come and get Jordan's ashes. He felt they belonged with me now because his life was over and his future was empty. This man has grown children, grandchildren, and great-grandchildren. I do not think his life is over. He has everything he needs. Grief works in mysterious ways.

I did not jump at the opportunity to go get Jordan's ashes because I had been forced to live without them for fourteen years. I had resigned myself to the fact that this man would keep them with him to the death. The last words he messaged me after he had moved away were ones of blame. I know I shouldn't let this bother me because, again, I know Jordan isn't there anymore. He isn't anywhere that I can see or touch him. It's the point of the matter, the grieving, the pain, and the loss, all rolled up together. I have forgiven Jordan's father because it's the right thing to do. Grudges take you nowhere in life, and the longer you hold onto them, the harder it is to let them go. Forgive, forget, and move on.

I will surely make the trip to get Jordan's ashes, when the timing is right. I would dearly love to have them. Maybe that's what my heart is waiting for. I would organize a ceremony, one he never had, and lay him to rest beside my father. Because Jordan has never been laid to rest, I feel like this whole thing is in limbo. Maybe this is why I feel so unsettled about the whole situation. I need closure. I need to grieve.

So I'll grieve tomorrow, whenever that day comes. I have deliberately put myself in the back seat for grieving. I have done this to myself, but I felt I had no other choice because of all the things I was dealing with at the time. The ignorant relation-ship I was in consumed my every emotional waking moment. My job demanded so much mental atten-tion and time that I clearly forgot to take for myself that I so deeply needed and deserved. I fell by the wayside by my own hands, and I am paying for it now. I am lost and broken.

So I will grieve tomorrow. I am at the point now where I ask myself, "When? When will tomorrow come?" I must find tomorrow to complete myself and my grief. I need closure on this open wound. I need to finally come to terms with my thoughts and emotions to do what my heart calls me to do. I cannot finish before I begin. I must confront the rest of my life and what it holds for me.

So I will grieve tomorrow, and when tomorrow comes, I will begin. I've been telling myself for fourteen years now that I will be okay, and it truly must be because somehow I am, except for the part of me that isn't. I know this makes no sense, but for the part of me that isn't cries out to be, to be finished, and to be acknowledged. Things left undone will never leave you alone.

I don't know what I will become or what miraculous changes will take place once I do find tomorrow. I do know that I shouldn't have waited so long to find closure and come to terms with the loss of my son's life. In all the years that he's been gone, I've always felt like there's this "something" in the back of my mind that I must do and that for now, this day, I will be okay. I've always told myself to carry on with life and do the things I have to do to get by. I will grieve tomorrow. I don't know what waits for me on the other side. I do know that my Jordan will still be gone, but I will have done that thing that beckons me on. If I don't, I will continue to pay for it.

I can barely give advice to a grieving parent about grief when clearly I have not. I pray there is some small shred of hope here in these pages that you can take to heart and know that someday we all will be okay. Don't wait to grieve! If there's something you feel that you need to do or someplace you need to be to gain some small piece of closure, do it. Take yourself out of the big picture for a while, and grieve your loss. Take care of your sadness. Cry, scream, laugh, or whatever it is you feel you need to do to express the emotions you are feeling. Please do it. You owe it to your child, and more importantly, you owe it to yourself. You deserve this. Child loss is devastating! It crushes you mentally, emotionally, and physically. Don't wait until tomorrow. Tomorrow may never come.

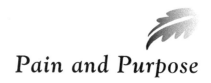

Pain and Purpose

With a bleeding heart, one that wants only to help and, maybe, ease a little of the pain and agony of child loss to parents, I say this, you are going to be okay, maybe not today or even tomorrow, maybe not even ten years from now down the road. Your pain is your pain, and however long it takes, take it. Don't rush the journey. Don't miss out on finding yourself and all that you are. Don't miss out on who you are becoming but rather love and embrace yourself along the way. Don't beat yourself up for the things you couldn't change. You are a living, breathing survivor, and you have a purpose. Small advancements in healing are going to take place in your lives that you may not even notice at first. The words "you're going to be okay" sound cruel coming from someone else, I know. I never thought I'd be saying them to myself, let alone have the guts to say them to someone I don't know. I guess there can be many different meanings to them depending on the source they come from. An outsider saying it might sound like he's saying, "Move on," or "Get over it." Truly, he may not mean it. This is not his world. He doesn't understand. If he hasn't walked in our shoes, he doesn't really know what it's like. It's not his fault. This is all he knows. Words can sound cold-hearted and uncaring when they are coming from a stranger to this type of grief. Their souls haven't been touched by this tragedy. We are in a class of our own, and my heart breaks knowing we won't be the last.

It will be a while before you feel good about yourself again, in your own skin. You are still you, only different. I know it's hard to keep your head above water, but you have people in your life, people looking out for you, and you still matter. You are still important. You matter to me. You are an integral part of creation, and you are enough. You need to tell yourself this every day. Be kind to yourself, and always, always take one day at a time. Scream, cry, yell, or do whatever it is you need to do. Don't hold it in. This is all a part of healing, and you need to express it. Don't hold anything back. Don't wait to grieve. Don't bottle it up. Put yourself first. I don't know your immediate circumstances, and you may have siblings of your child in your home. I realize and understand this, but do not forget you! Take care of yourself, for them.

When I say to myself I'm going to be okay, waves of sadness wash over me because I know I must move on, and I realize that I have moved on just enough to be able to say these words. I know I cannot stay where I've been, in a pit of pain. I am still a productive member of society, whereas in the past, I was not, but there will always be a part of me that wants to go back, back to the sadness and pain because that's where my Jordan is, or so my brain thinks. I think that's what we all want, to go back to those first crucial days because of the what-ifs and whys. We think that somehow, we could have changed things. There was that one second in time that took the life of our child, and the anxiety will linger on. Truth be told, my son's memory lives within me, and nothing will ever change that. I must move on, and the memory of him will go with me. I've grown enough to realize that and that he will always be a part of me. No matter what. I hold on to that. I thank God each day for all the days and years I had Jordan. My heart and soul miss him incredibly, and that creates anxiety within myself because of what I cannot have. I would take him back in a heartbeat, but I know that's not possible. I cannot turn back time, and the world will not stop turning.

To you, dear fellow grieving parent, it appears nothing is possible anymore. Your whole world has been turned upside down and dramatically changed forever. That's a fact. Nothing in your life will ever again be the same. You won't be the same. Every day now seems to be a struggle and saps you of your strength. Just remind yourself to breathe. Existing now is the most important thing you can do. Life is calling up strength from you to make it through to the next day, and the day after that, a strength you didn't know you had will surface. I pray you find your way on this journey. Take one day at a time, one breath at a time, and embrace yourself and love yourself. There is no map or manual for this road you are on. We are all different in our own special way but share a bond, an unseen one that holds us all together. We didn't ask for or sign up for this, but I know we will make it through. Each of us must find the way that works best.

Time Never-Ending

The river of time will continue to gently flow throughout eternity and carry with it all that has happened to me and what I have been through. It will never rest. As I lay down my head each night, a blanket of ghosts from the past and future covers me. In the solitude of darkness, there is no longer anyone to hide from. I close my eyes, and I thank God for my son. He had a big part in who I am today, and I wouldn't have traded him or the life we had together for anything. Jordan was the light of my life, my best friend, and my reason for living. My mother always said, "Your life's not complete until you have a child." I had a child. My child died. I am complete no more. I am undone. I was left asking myself the question, "What am I now?" There was just this big empty space in my soul, a hole in my heart that left me wondering, *What do I do now?* Pain and suffering take complete control of your life, your every waking moment. Who am I now? How do I live now that Jordan is gone? How do I cope with all of this? How in the hell am I going to go on? There were just too many questions with not enough answers. I didn't even know where to find them. These were all questions that I should never have had to ask myself. This wasn't how life was supposed to go. I do know this to be true; the day I gave Jordan back, the day I let him go and gave him back to God, is the day I felt some peace and comfort of a promise that I would see him again. These questions are just pieces of me that I must work through on my journey. Giving him back did not make it all go away, but it gave me something to look forward to. It gave me something to work with. I wanted to hang on to Jordan forever, more so than when he was alive. I didn't want to let him go; it hurt like hell that day, but he was already gone. My heart just didn't know it. When the thought of that day goes through my mind, it takes a detour straight to my heart and pains me so. I still think of how horribly, unbelievably wrong it is that my boy is dead. When you must face that fact repeatedly, it truly is mind-boggling. Reminding yourself, and your heart, every day that your child is gone is like ripping a scab off a wound and then watching it bleed —everyday! When will my heart accept the facts? It is something that I don't want to be true. My heart is incapable of processing this information.

I live with the fear of my son's memory moving too far away from me. With each passing day, which turns into years, I fear I will forget things about him if I don't think about him enough. I replay loving moments in my mind. The kind, loving person he was soothes my mind, and I thank God I still have that. The sound of his voice has always been import-ant to me and how I remember it. I have fears he will disappear from me forever. I know that can never happen. He is still a huge part of me. I would have given my last breath to save his beautiful life.

Jordan lived a good, clean life and was a big-hearted young man. He didn't always know what he wanted to do with his life, and by the time he discovered what it was he did want, he was taken. He cared deeply for others and showed his compassion often. I was so proud of him for all he did. These things I know will live on as part of his legacy and stay in my heart and mind forever. I miss him so much. Sometimes, I think I will just crack open, and the sadness inside of me will all spill out that, at times, gets the better of me. How can there be so much sadness and tears inside one person? There are times I wonder, as we all do, I'm sure, why him? I know I've said this before, but why him? I want answers. The answers to that question, ultimately, I have come to realize, do not exist. I want to scream and yell at God above for some sort of explanation. I know this is not the answer either.

I believe each human has a God-given purpose, and it is our job to figure out what that purpose is. Some of us spend our whole lives wondering why we are here on this planet. Being lost in this life cannot be the reason. I'm praying this is mine because I don't have it in me to go searching for another purpose. I thought when Jordan was alive that he was my purpose, to be his mom. So I lived my life being his mommy, and all was good. Now that he's gone, writing these words down and knowing this is something I must do feel like the only purpose I have left for a living since he's gone. I feel like this book has already been written. I only needed to be reminded of it. Like the pages of our lives in the book of life, we need a gentle reminder.

The metaphor I use, grass grows in winter, means to me that I will survive this tragedy. It means that I will be okay. With God watching over me and guiding me, how can I not? Grass can bear the weight and stresses of the harshest of seasons. It gets blanketed and buried each winter under many feet of heavy snowfall. Grass can freeze underneath that snow or with just a frost, and yet it comes back with a dapple of sunlight. Grass survives fires, floods, and hailstorms and yet does not wither away. It comes back stronger and healthier than before it was attacked. Grass grows in winter, and if you remove the covers of snow from above it, you will see it is still alive. It is still beautiful.

I'll say it again, and I know no one wants someone telling them they'll be okay, especially after their child has died. It almost feels like someone is saying it with disregard to what has happened to them, like they are just ruthlessly brushing aside your pain. Your pain is your pain, and you must let that someone know that's not what you need to hear right now. There will be a time for that. Your heart and mind just cannot take that in right now. I pray, though, dear reader, that in time, you will be able to say these words to yourself, just maybe not right now: I'm going to be okay. The memories and love you hold dearly in your heart for your child will never go away. It is with you in all that you do, day and night. He or she will always be a precious part of you, forever, and no one or anything could ever change that. Of this, I am certain. Replay the memories you hold so dearly repeatedly in your mind. This may bring sadness but also comfort. Be proud of the person you made. He will live on inside of you forever, and in time maybe, smiles and joy will come instead of tears and sadness. Although the latter may still come at times and unexpectedly, I pray for happiness, in just knowing that your child's memory grows within you more and more. I pray the good Lord brings you more good days than bad. Your child was a light to this world and a most important part of creation. He or she was here for a reason. Your child was special to you, and the world needs to know she existed. We may no longer be complete and still lost, but this isn't about change overnight. It's about gradually finding ourselves in this new world we live in and creating a plan that works best for us, one we can live with. This, too, takes time, and as time goes by, I find that somehow things start to fall into place. When I see progress happening in my own life, I feel the urge to go backward. At that very moment, I discovered I had made a change. A part of me wants to stay in the raw grief I experienced and lived in when Jordan first died, as if he was still there. The heart wants what the heart wants. This tells me I have grown. I know I must move forward with my life, forward to the next chapter. I haven't left Jordan behind. He's still with me in spirit, and yes, I did let him go, but not the parts I still need, the parts that will always be with me, living inside of me. These are the pieces that survived. These are the pieces that keep me going, that and the fact that I will see him again. For now, my life is a little less jumbled up and strewn about the pages. I am still broken and probably always will be because a huge part of me is gone, but I am a little more organized now and growing. I will survive. I will be okay.

Compassion-Filled Life

When I look into the eyes of another whose child has died, I can see their pain. I can see through their smiles. It's like I am looking back at myself. I have to wonder about the circumstances, and I don't ask, but sometimes, they will tell their story. I think about what's going on inside of me and wonder how they are getting through their grief or if they are at all. Do they have anyone to talk to? Do they have a support system? Do they have anyone in their life that really cares and is there for them when their grief spills out of them? It's a hard thing to know just by how they talk. I know that I keep a lot bottled up inside and go for very long periods of time without ever talking to anyone about Jordan. I hold him close to my heart every day though. It's strange; I am afraid to lose him, although I already have. One of my biggest fears now is that I will forget the sound of his voice. One of the things he said, "I love you, Mommy," runs through my mind, and it sounds like him, and I can go on for another day. I recall that voice, and I know it is his. It's like a feeling of reassurance, somehow, that he is still with me. He is still near to my heart. This is part of what keeping his memory alive means to me. I have not seen him physically for all these years, and it seems he is so far away that I can just bring him back by the sound of his voice. I know this isn't much, but for this mom, it's a form of comfort in a world of turmoil.

Living is a hard thing to do when your child has died. I felt like my purpose for living was over, like I had no reason to even be here anymore. It was like nothing I did up to this point was worth anything. I had no reason to *be*. Of course, I wanted out of this misery. It took a lot of years to realize that I had to stay here. Dying was not the answer, and it certainly wasn't going to bring Jordan back. Not in all eternity here on earth would I see him again. I knew I had to stop being so negative and angry all the time and accept his death. None of the negativity I was feeling was doing any good to me. I wanted to be happy once again and get back into my life. Instead of rejecting the fact that Jordan was dead, I started to embrace it. I had no other choice, and it certainly didn't mean I was happy with it, by no means. That could never be. I turned my pain into my purpose. My purpose is to gently and lovingly tell other parents that they will survive this. I know that no one wants to hear this. There's not one parent who wants another telling them that they're going to be okay, especially one who has not walked in their shoes, but I have. We just want to lie down and literally wallow in our grief. I've been there, and no one can tell me it's going to be okay because that's a big fat lie. This is what we all think: that it's not going to be okay.

We are going to feel the impact of this death for the rest of our lives. Our child will always be gone from our sight and side. I know that each of us bears horrible pain that we wouldn't wish upon anyone, not even our worst enemy (if we had one). I know that we pretend all through the day that we are fine and nothing is wrong. There are days we will burst open with tears if someone looks at us with that caring look. I go to work some days and wait for one person who is going to make a comment about a child or ask if I have any children. I know this is so hard, but instead of dropping my heart on the floor, I'm going to say yes and brag about how great my son was but that he's not with us anymore. If someone asks you about your child, tell them, yes, they lived a great life. Tell them all about him or her. Lift their life up, and feel good doing it. Your child was here. Your child existed. Your child was a great person. When we are finally able to do this, a spark of "I think I am going to be okay" surfaces. These are the things that we feel good about.

I have let grief and sadness rule over me for so long that, to tell you the truth, I am tired. I am tired of being depressed. I am tired of this burden, although I will carry it through life. I want to be okay again. Grief is a heavy burden to carry alone. I believe it's such a personal load that each of us carries it differently. Carry it with honor and pride. Embrace your child's life for the time they were here. You were number one in their lives. You and they matter.

Teardrops on My Heart

I'll let you go but for a while
The sky's so bright—I'll see a smile
And then the sun, the rays of light
Come down like shards to sway the night
The dawn it stays to light your way
The path it seems is worn and gray
Your home's not far from where you trod
Your resting place to be with God
He welcomes you with outstretched arms
He cradles you with nail-scarred palms
Calls you His own, His own come home
Rest in His light, don't fear the night
Till we meet again my child
I'll let you go but for a while

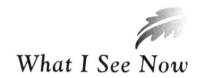

What I See Now

I sat and watched the sun go down
 And I saw you there
I took a drive where wildflowers grow
 And I saw you there
I drove by a fishing hole, it beckoned us to come
 And I saw you there
I saw majestic mountains covered in snow
 And I saw you there
I stopped by some old friends' house just to say Hello
 And I saw you there
I took a drive through forests of green
 And I saw you there
I saw elk and deer elude the hunter
 And I saw you there
I went on a hike to a pristine mountain lake
 And I saw you there
I went to church to worship our Lord
 And I saw you there
I looked into the faces of our family and friends
 And I saw you there
I looked at the lives that you have touched
 And I saw you there

I looked at the night sky full of stars
    And I saw you there
I looked all around at all I could see
    And I saw you there
I looked at the person who I am today
    And I saw you there
I looked in my heart and the love that's inside
    And I saw you there

Leftover Love

I save all my tears for the times I'm alone
I let them fall from my heart
Like raindrops from a storm
They tell the story of the way I feel
This mother's love for her child
Is spinning like a wheel

I held him close in my arms
Rocked him to sleep
Kissed away all his worries
In the times that he felt weak
He grew into a fine young man
Had the world in his hands

Now he's gone and time moves on
What do I do with this leftover love

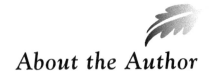

About the Author

Cheryl Williams grew up in North Idaho where she currently resides with her mother. There are a lot of things her mother can no longer do, so they help each other out. Her greatest accomplishment was being a mother. She is currently employed at a small convenience store and enjoys the great outdoors (driving through the mountains, picking huckleberries, and hunting) and spending time with family. She is a first-time author, a writer of poetry, and loves to paint. She has deep compassion for helping others through this thing called grief.